DRONES

SUSAN HENNEBERG

D0711246

red rhino
b**OO**k s®
NONFICTION

Area 51

Cannibal Animals

Cloning

Drones

Fault Lines

Great Spies of the World

Hacked

Monsters of the Deep

Monsters on Land

Seven Wonders of the Ancient World

Tuskegee Airmen

Virtual Reality

Witchcraft

Wormholes

SADDLEBACK
EDUCATIONAL PUBLISHING
www.sdlback.com

All source images from Shutterstock.com

ISBN-13: 978-1-68021-029-3
ISBN-10: 1-68021-029-7
eBook: 978-1-63078-336-5

Printed in Malaysia

20 19 18 17 16   2 3 4 5 6

TABLE OF CONTENTS

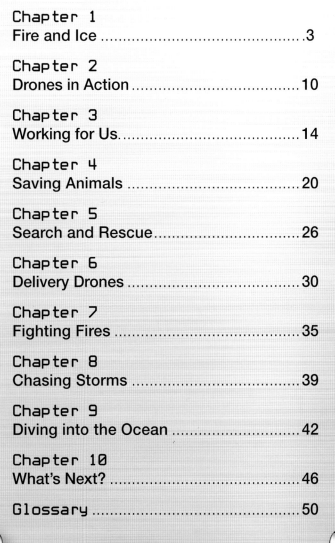

Chapter 1
FIRE AND ICE

It is dark out.

But you can see a red glow.

Boom!

Fire shoots up. Sparks fly.

Hot lava flows down a sheet of ice.

It is a *volcano*.

It is erupting in Iceland.

Iceland has many volcanoes.

They *erupt* often.

The lava is hot. It burns the land.

It makes ice melt.

That is a problem.

Mud flows. Towns flood.

Houses fall. People have to move.

People want to know more.

But no one can get close.

The lava is too hot.

The air is bad to breathe.

ICELAND

Eric Cheng flew to Iceland in 2014.

He had an idea.

People could not get close to the volcano.

But he had something that could.

Cheng drove near the volcano.

Then he hiked in closer.

He wore a gas mask.

The air was bad.

It was full of hot dust.

He sent up a small *helicopter*.

It had a camera on it.

The copter flew to the volcano.

It got close. It filmed the lava.

Cheng tracked it on his phone.

But then something went wrong.

He could not see the copter.

Cheng waited.

Then he heard a sound.

The copter came back.

The camera had melted.

But the SD card was fine.

The film was safe.

Cheng had video of the volcano.

He could show it to others.

Chapter 2

DRONES IN ACTION

What is this small helicopter?

Does it fly by itself?

It is a *drone*.

It works by *remote control*.

No one is on board.

A person flies it using a smartphone.

Drones like Cheng's have another name.

Unmanned Aerial Vehicles.

They are called UAVs.

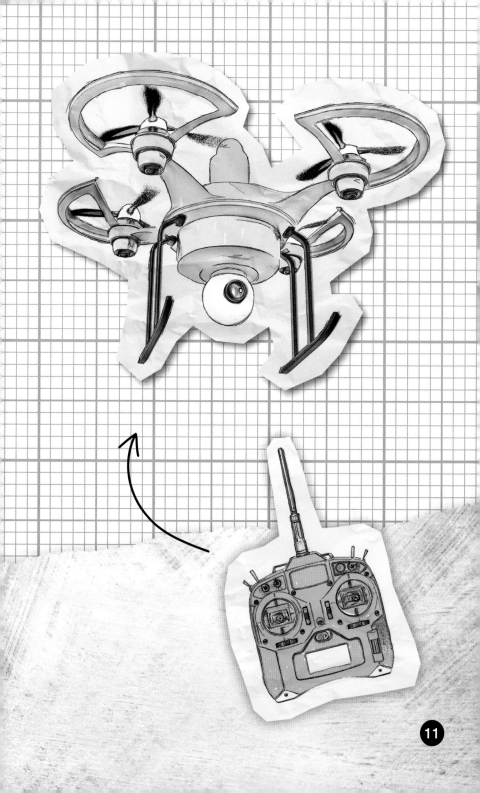

Drones come in many sizes.

Some are big.

They look like planes.

These drones fly.

They have wings.

Wings give them lift.

DRONE DATA

Eric Cheng used a drone with four blades. It is called a quad-copter.

Some drones are small.

They may look like toy helicopters.

These drones have blades.

The blades spin fast.

The spin lifts the drone.

Some drones are tiny.

They are as small as bugs.

They look like bees.

They have wings that beat fast.

BEE DRONE

Chapter 3
WORKING FOR US

Drones have a lot of uses.
They go where we cannot.

They see inside volcanoes.
Spy for us in war.
Save wild animals.
Find lost hikers.
Track wildfires.
Watch storms.
Dive into the ocean.

Drones were first used in war.
The U.S. Army used them in the
1960s and 1970s.
The U.S. was at war in Asia.
It needed spies.
Drones could do the job.
And no one got hurt.

The first Army UAVs were big planes.
They held cameras.
They filmed the land.
They found the enemy.
The Army could plan attacks.
Drones were their *scouts*.

Drones are still used in war.
They fly to war zones.
They find the enemy.

The drones are quiet.
They are fast.
They fly under radar.
Some hold bombs.

Who pilots these drones?
Experts fly them using computers.
They use *GPS* to guide the UAVs.
They see what the drones see.
They learn about the enemy.
Drones help win wars.

DRONE DATA

The U.S Department of Defense has
spent billions of dollars on UAVs.

Chapter 4
SAVING ANIMALS

Drones may be war spies.
But they spy on other things too.
People are using them to help animals.

Some animals are *endangered*.
Laws protect them.
But *poachers* hunt them.
They hide.
They shoot the animals when
no one is looking.
They need to be stopped.
But who can catch them?
Drones can.

LION SKINS ARE SOLD
ON THE BLACK MARKET

Africa is one place where drones are helping.

Lions are hunted there.

People want their skins.

The poachers also hunt rhinos.

They want their tusks.

They can sell the skins and tusks.

DRONE DATA

Some drones have night vision. They can find poachers in the dark.

Poachers are good at hiding.

No one can see them.

They think no one can stop them.

But that is changing.

Some drones look like birds.

These drones film poachers.

They catch them in the act.

Drones also film hard-to-find animals.
Orangutans live in Asia.
They are a kind of ape.
They live in trees.
They build nests in them.
They sleep there.

The trees are hard to get to.
They are on very steep hills.
Their leaves are thick.
The apes are hard to find.
But drones can find them.
They can take pictures.
Some show orangutan nests.
We learn more about these apes.

DRONES FLY OVER TREES

Chapter 5
SEARCH AND RESCUE

Drones save people too.

They can be used to search.

They can see in rain and snow.

They can see in the dark.

This helps them find lost hikers.

How does a drone search?

It flies over hiking paths.

It films the land.

It can see body heat.

This is how it finds people.

Rescue workers look at the films.

They know where to search.

Lost people are found.

DRONE DATA

Many people own drones. Some want
to use their drones to help find lost
people. They offer to help local search
and rescue teams.

Hurt hikers need to be found fast.
But it takes time to find them.
A drone can speed up the search.
How?

Drones fly over hills.
They film the ground.
The films are put online.

Anyone can look.
Anyone can help.

Searchers look for clues.
They tag pictures online.
A map shows the tags.
Lost hikers are tagged.
They are found.

Chapter 6
DELIVERY DRONES

Drones can help people who are sick.

How?

They can deliver *medicine*.

Haiti is an island.

In 2010 there was an *earthquake*.

It was a bad one.

Many people died. Even more were hurt.

Houses fell. Roads broke.

No one could drive.

No one could get to towns.

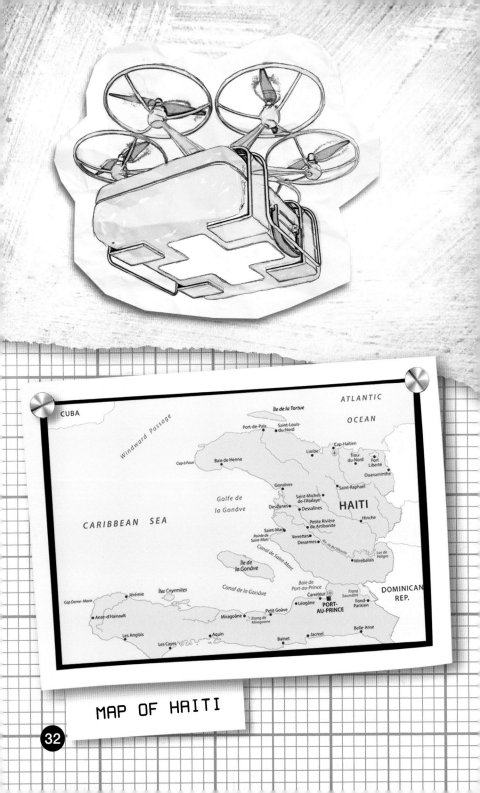

MAP OF HAITI

Some roads are still blocked today.
But drones don't need roads.
They need air space.
They need a place to land.

Experts tested drones in Haiti.
The tests worked.
Drones got to the towns.
They brought medicine.
Sick people got help.

Another test was done in 2014.

A company delivered medicine to an island.

The island is part of Germany.

But it is far out at sea.

DRONE DATA

Delivery drones are being tested around the world. Some companies want to use drones to deliver things people order online.

Chapter 7

FIGHTING FIRES

Drones can fly over fires.
They can help firefighters.

Fighting fires is hard.
It is full of danger.
Firefighters need good *data*.
Where is the fire? How fast is it?
How hot? Will it jump a road?
Will it burn houses?

It is hard to see in a fire.

There is thick smoke.

But some firefighters are using a new tool.

They carry small drones.

The drones can fly above a fire.

They can film.

They can put data on maps.

Firefighters have smartphones.

The phones show the films.

They show the maps.

Firefighters can learn about the fire.

Firefighters also use large drones.

These drones carry water.

They can fly over forest fires.

They can drop water.

They can help put fires out.

Chapter 8
CHASING STORMS

Storms can be deadly.
Strong winds blow.
The winds can knock down trees.
They can knock down houses.

Experts want to learn about storms.
Knowing more helps them *predict*
what storms will do.

Experts can't fly near a storm.

It is too risky.

But a drone can.

It can fly over the storm.

It can see down.

It can go inside a storm.

Some drones drop *probes*.

Probes are small tools.

They fall into the storm.

They send data.

Experts read the data.

They learn how cold the storm is.

They find the speed.

This tells them where the storm is going.

People can be warned.

They have time to get to a safe place.

Chapter 9

DIVING INTO THE OCEAN

The ocean is deep.

We do not know much about its floor.

It is hard to go down that far.

It is not safe for divers.

But drones can go.

They dive like subs.

They film things no one has seen before.

Ocean drones can get close to animals.

They film fish. They film whales and sharks.

But drones do more than take pictures.

They collect data too.

They look for changes in the ocean.

Is there more acid in the water?

Is it warmer? Is ice melting?

MELTING ICE IS
DANGEROUS FOR ANIMALS

Drones find cracks in the ocean floor.
The cracks are in the earth's *crust*.

Drones film the cracks.
They map them.
Some drones have arms.
They grab rocks. They scoop sand.

Drones can be our eyes in the ocean.

They can find planes that crashed.

They can find ships that sank.

They can go inside the wrecks.

Look for clues.

Chapter 10

WHAT'S NEXT?

Experts have many plans for drones.
Some will be fun.

Here is one idea.

You go out with friends.

Drones wait on you in a café.

Serve your food. Play you music.

Drones do the work. You relax.

Do you think that will happen?

There are more drones every year.

People use them for fun.

Drones film fireworks.

They fly above races.

They take pictures people cannot.

So why don't we see more drones?

Not everyone wants them.

People worry about *privacy*.

No one wants to be spied on.

Flying drones can be trouble too.

They can fall and hit people.

They can fly too high.

That can get in the way of big planes.

CLOSE-UP OF A DRONE

The U.S. is working on rules.

So are other countries.

The rules will say how drones can be used.

Now is a good time to work with drones.

Learn all you can.

Drones are not just toys.

They can do things we cannot.

How will we use them?

You will help decide.

GLOSSARY

aerial: in the sky

crust: the outer layer of the earth's surface

data: facts and numbers put together to learn about something

drone: a machine with no one on board; it is moved by remote control

earthquake: a sudden and violent shaking of the earth

endangered: at risk of going away for good

erupt: to burst out lava and ash

GPS: global positioning satellite

helicopter: an aircraft that flies by using spinning blades

medicine: drugs given by doctors to help sick people get well

orangutan: an ape that lives in trees; it has long, red hair and long arms

poacher: a person who hunts animals illegally

predict: say what will happen in the future

privacy: being apart from other people; not being seen or watched

probe: a small machine used to measure or test something

remote control: moved by someone far away

scout: a person or aircraft sent ahead of an army to learn about the enemy

unmanned: no one in the vehicle

vehicle: a thing used to move people or things from one place to another

volcano: a mountain or hill with a hole in the earth where lava flows out

TAKE A LOOK INSIDE

WORMHOLES

Chapter 1
A GALAXY FAR AWAY

Three! Two! One!
Blast off!
The rocket roars.
Slowly it climbs into the sky.
It rattles.
It shakes.

Upward.
Higher!
Faster!

The sky turns colors.
First blue.
Then violet.
Now black.

We can't see gravity.
Still, we know it's there.
Grab a book.
Let it go.
The book falls.
Gravity is at work.

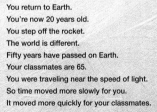

Gravity may have created wormholes too.
Imagine if it did.
We may have a way to explore the universe.
We may go places people only dream of.

Chapter 9
TIME TRAVEL

Time travel is tricky.
Some scientists study time.
They have found something interesting.
Time is not always the same.
It slows down as things move faster.
We don't see that on Earth.
We can't travel fast enough.

But a rocket in space might be fast enough.
Let's say you are 15.
You leave Earth in a spaceship.
It moves almost as fast as light.
You travel for five years.
At least it was five years for you.

You return to Earth.
You're now 20 years old.
You step off the rocket.
The world is different.
Fifty years have passed on Earth.
Your classmates are 65.
You were traveling near the speed of light.
So time moved more slowly for you.
It moved more quickly for your classmates.

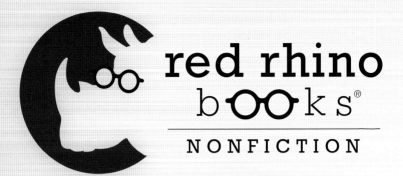

red rhino b**oo**ks®

NONFICTION

9781680210293

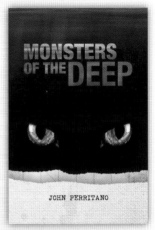

9781680210286

9781680210309

9781680210330

VIRTUAL
REALITY
JOHN PERRITANO

9781680210361

CAROL PIXLEY

Witchcraft

9781680210323

AREA 51

T. J. HANSEN

9781680210316

FAULT
LINES

JOHN PERRITANO

9781680210538

CLONING

SUSAN HENNEBERG

9781680210347

SEVEN
WONDERS
of ANCIENT WORLD

ARIANNE McHUGH

9781680210354

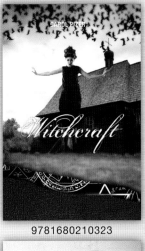